DODGING BULLIES

poems by

Charles Becker

Finishing Line Press
Georgetown, Kentucky

DODGING BULLIES

Copyright © 2023 by Charles Becker
ISBN 979-8-88838-092-5 First Edition
All rights reserved under International and Pan-American Copyright Conventions. No part of this book may be reproduced in any manner whatsoever without written permission from the publisher, except in the case of brief quotations embodied in critical articles and reviews.

ACKNOWLEDGMENTS

Versions of some of these poems were previously published in literary journals, anthologies, or books. Thanks to the editors.

Arroyo Arts Collective Poetry in the Windows V: "Haiku"
Beginnings Publishing: "Midsummer's Day"
The Dandelion Review: "My Hero"
Grenadier Press, *My Life is Poetry Anthology*: "Out at The Beach"
Orchard Street Press: "Yoga Before Bed"
Oyster River Pages: "Being the One;" "He's The One (They Don't Know I'm Your Boyfriend)"
Passager Journal: "Out West"
Rush Magazine, Mount St. Mary's University Press: "After Our Nap"
Switchgrass Review: "The Soup We Give"
World Stage Press: *Friends My Poems Gave Me*: "Photo Portrait;" "Prom Date;"
"What We Believe;" "What We Know;" "Snow, 1992;" "Birthday;" "End Poem"

Many of these poems were created in workshops and classes.
Thanks to these instructors:
Steven Reigns, The LGBT Center, Los Angeles: My Life is Poetry Workshops
Hiram Sims, The Community Literature Initiative, Los Angeles
Carol Celucci, Barnsdall Art Center, Los Angeles

Publisher: Leah Huete de Maines
Editor: Christen Kincaid
Cover Art: Charles Becker
Author Photo: Charles Becker
Cover Design: Elizabeth Maines McCleavy

Order online: www.finishinglinepress.com
also available on amazon.com

Author inquiries and mail orders:
Finishing Line Press
PO Box 1626
Georgetown, Kentucky 40324
USA

Table of Contents

Haiku 1

This Child 2

Photo Portrait 3

Road Trip 4

For A Kingdom 5

My Hero 7

Best Friend 9

What We Believe 10

Birthday 12

The One 13

Prom Date 14

Ma Vie en Rose 15

Out at the Beach 16

My Blended Self 17

Famous 19

Midsummer's Day 20

Being the One 21

Snow 1992 22

The Soup We Give 24

He's The One (They Don't Know I'm Your Boyfriend) 26

After Our Nap 28

Yoga At Bedtime 30

Out West 32

What We Know 34

This Adult 35

End 36

Haiku

The children laughing
boy who is not included
hears them all his life

THIS CHILD

If he grows up that way, I wonder if he'll ever be liked
his quiet voice makes him stand out but be invisible, too,
he promises he'll be good, though, vigilant and perfectly good.

PHOTO PORTRAIT

I am 5 years old. I have blond hair and a cleft in my chin. My father likes taking snapshots and I do what I am told. There is a neighbor's dog. His name is Pal. He is blind and today I am posed petting his head. I squint my eyes in the sunlight. I wear saddle shoes and shorts. My socks are brown. The neighbor's house smells like cigarettes and canned dog food. I do what I am told. I hold my breath, smile, and feel sorry for blind dogs. As the camera flashes I expect to disappear forever. My legs are bare. My arms are always covered. I am shy and never say no. I squint my eyes in the sunlight.

ROAD TRIP

Sometimes I create
memories
from photographs
but this time
I was truly there
small and quiet
safe with my brother and sister
in the back seat of our Plymouth.
We had started out early
before dawn
and soon afterwards stopped
for breakfast at the side
of the road, mother cooking
food with her portable stove
bacon and eggs grilled
together on grandmother's
black frying pan. Gradually
what I remember wanting
was to simply stay
where we were
forever, the grassy roadside
as final destination, greenness
frozen into still life, and me
never having to get back
inside the car, because just then
everyone belonged together
and the day was only beginning
to show light
in its embracing silence.

FOR A KINGDOM

Little C.B. howls in third grade
hasn't got the words
he runs and runs, he wants to be
a bullfrog
longs to have best friends
joy to the world
all these boys and girls
joy to the children in their deep blue
see
see
schools are made
for straight kids
sit down
do the work
be quiet
oh run, C.B., please run

gay boys are bad, his teachers say
he bolts, he jolts
he needs a one-on-one
at eight years old
watch this story fast unfold
and see him come undone

now I lay me down to sleep
to sleep, to dream, to play
come out, come out
whoever you are
C. be nimble, C. be quick
I'll huff and I'll puff
I'll blow your hurt away

I say, talk
talk to me, inner
child, tell me what you know
your eyes are full of places
a kid should never go
you need to speak your truth
don't run, bright student

Candy Land is your game
I'll help you learn
the feel of win
without the nameless
shame.
You'll skip, you'll hop
the colorful trail
eat your gumdrops
on the way, you'll
kick Lord Licorice
in the face
your demons just can't stay
not real, they're shadows
disillusions
friend, you're safe
your turn, just choose
one card
this card and move
ahead, King Kandy waits
with fattened cheeks
leap, leaps to keep
what's true
you gain because you play
   you always could
   you always should
   without fear
   without blame

Star light, star bright
I wish you may
I wish you might
might
mighty power
use these words
all day
and through the night
they're yours
to say
you matter
you matter
I matter.

MY HERO

I wanted biceps
big like yours
with a hula girl tattoo
who danced when I flexed
and mighty forearms of steel
real threats to the bullies
who chased and haunted me.
I wanted your strength
your rich green spinach, I'd watch
you squeeze open
the can with your bare, macho hand
swallow it all in one gulp
and then take Brutus down
without sweating a drop
or losing your gritty grin
scratchy, manly chuckle.
I wanted your punch, Popeye, I needed
you to teach me self-defense, I longed
to be your forever buddy.

Puff, too, he lived by the sea
and did magic tricks for little boys
the way dragons can. We, fearless, frolicked
in the autumn mist
best friends, and sailed free on billowed
boats, far from taunts or cuts of mean kids
who didn't care for fantasy fun
or innocence.
I needed you, Puff, your spiked tail
your commanding roar
for myself each time I left home
thinking I was all alone.

Sure, I lived the life of Superman
long before I knew Clark Kent
me, growing into a secret
not a bird, not a plane
steeling my face, hiding what no superpower
could fix or overcome.

I needed you, Superman, your rock-square
chin, your smiling sureness, when my world
where cowboys fell in love
with other cowboys, seemed
in danger of being crushed.
But in the end, I found
you, mortal imperfect
Fred Rogers, me, hopelessly
fearful, like Daniel Striped Tiger, wondering
where my next breath would ever come from.
Mr. Rogers, you welcomed me
into your neighborhood
looked me in the eye
and said I made your day
a special one
just by being me.
I put on your cardigan
wore your navy Keds
and took from you
a voice
your voice
softly sincere
for my own
whenever I might need it.

BEST FRIEND

Because the summer
lake was ours
we liked to swim
in its deepest end
where afternoon shade
helped hide
our shriveled
blue toes, hairless
white legs
kicking and flipping
like imaginary
amphibian selves
though teenagers
we breathed there
July and August
keeping our heads
at water
level
knowing land
would call us
soon enough
and we'd surely
be teased
shamed again
for being
that word
queer.

WHAT WE BELIEVE

Bullies are assholes. I mean
when I was 13, I was scared of bullies,
the white ones with crewcuts and freckles
the ones who wore cowboy boots and tight pants
the ones who threw the ball so hard
it stung my hand, the ones
who laughed when I swung the bat
and missed, the ones
who spit

the ones who smoked and didn't cough
the ones who never carried books
and spoke with raspy voices, put their hands
under girlfriends' shirts
drove and drank beer

the ones who roamed the streets in packs
and terrorized day dreamers
stunning their senses
so they could never find a way back
or belong anywhere again.

Sometimes I was afraid of God
most times I was hurt
I never said a word.
I came to believe in strange things
how if I could just be good enough
how everyone else knew the truth
how butterflies and lightning bugs
could live in a jar
if I punctured holes through the lid
and gave them sweet flowers to eat.

At night I would listen for the sound of mist
sinking into tree branches, jacarandas
growing crown-shaped purple buds
over the streets, the quiet calm of cotton sheets
coaxing sleep above my body's skin.
I would count fingerprints posing
on cold, clear windows, breathe

warm circles from my mouth, make friends
with my heartbeat, anything
to make me feel safe
anything

BIRTHDAY

I am sixteen
years old when
my father decides
to change jobs, move
the family to Ohio. I beg
to stay behind but get packed
with suitcases, boxes of utensils.
All windows are closed as we drive
away. The trip is endless mountains and
cities I already hate for their factories, smoke
and gray faces. In Columbus my father stops to
ask for directions, it is summer and hot. Old men
in overalls ask why we are moving. I don't speak, I
am the invisible good boy. Days later at my new school
I am the strange kid with the Jersey accent. Outcasts among
sweet girls are drawn to my shyness but for the bullies I am an
edible target. The insults eat me alive like a wolf's afternoon snack.
One day in study hall the teacher is late. Circling my desk, a pack of
greasers calls me four eyes, bookworm, faggot. A drop of spit falls onto
my homework. There is blood at its center. Like the cornered animal my
body stiffens and prepares to die, hoping this time will become the very last.

THE ONE

I was the one, though I willed myself invisible at seventeen over and over I was
the one asked for spare change as I walked to school, the one shamed at face
so ambushed I'd give away my lunch, rainbowed notebooks, colored pens
for ransom. I was the one, like a dog waiting with ball in mouth, blind
devoted to its master, standing still waiting for permission to play or
speak. I was the one with a secret, like the first thing I was seemed
the worst thing to be, spoke quiet, loved to sing, read long novels
whispered words from poems, cried silent at romance films and
knew all the lines, planted seeds in paper cups to grow lilacs by
kitchen windows, set tables in hope of fancy dinners, ironed
shirts and darned my own socks. I was the one who loved
and wanted to be loved by other boys, at prom danced
in my mind with cute guys and fashioned a rhinestone
evening bag, tinsel on my scented lips, and still
dreamed of being someone else more macho.

PROM DATE

I didn't quite know what to do, when the breathy rustle of her fuchsia mermaid sweetheart floor-length beaded taffeta dress, and her silk with crystal rhinestones evening bag, satin stiletto, closed-toe platform pumps accented by faux-ruby flowers, her short-sleeve lace special occasion wrap, plus her grandmother's crescent-shaped diamond broach like a jeweled June moon cradled between the hint of her lightly glittered cleavage, and my sudden crimson rush of jealousy when her father kissed her goodbye, all made me realize I wanted so much more to wear her outfit to prom rather than my own pointless, powder-blue tuxedo and understated, pleats-up cummerbund.

MA VIE EN ROSE

When I come out I will be the real deal
a steal, one Happy Meal congealed

as much as mac and cheese or Cantonese
vegetables and spice, refried beans

one lean machine in between parties
a sacred, scratched out catnap after party

nights rapped and snapped, a psychic
healing feeling and kneeling, reeling

in the catch, a match I made from heaven
a sleeper, a keeper, one holy roller

fashion patroller, out of controller
unique, speaking deeper, seeking softer

in a place where I recognize each face
of the sky and it knows mine.

When I come out I will be in bold ink
exaggerated pink connecting links

syncing clumsy grateful sex with love
and friends and truth. My coming out

is a breathing full, laughing loud
talking slow, gushing blushing touching

all that's new, it's a being outraged
smashing closet doors, a howling

holding hands, expanding, standing still
for the first time in my life, a growing

living in my own self surrounded by friends
who spent years seeking each other and found me.

OUT AT THE BEACH

That Saturday night, when bedtime wanted someone else
I went fishing under the pier
cast my line into a cold Pacific darkness
waited for gestures, a nod

I went fishing under the pier
shoulder to shoulder like salmon spawn upstream
waited for gestures, a nod
without words in an ocean of men

shoulder to shoulder like salmon spawn upstream
you bragged straight teeth, puffed big cheeks
without words in an ocean of men
I was lured to lick salt from your pores

you bragged straight teeth, puffed big cheeks
whiskered nibbles pulled at my grip, unbalanced me
I was lured to lick salt from your pores
iridescent drops of sea inside wet mouths

whiskered nibbles pulled at my grip, unbalanced me
we moved together like a school of Romeos
iridescent drops of sea inside wet mouths
our bodies whirled tidepools, coastal foams surged

we moved like a school of Romeos
hooked through lips and tongues
our bodies whirled tidepools, coastal foams surged
that Saturday night, when bedtime wanted someone else

MY BLENDED SELF

A muscular elongated hand
or foot
touches you, detached
cool at first, a pure
ice cube turquoise
drawn to embody
symmetry
then follow
and cross the line
from aloof to seduced.
Women wonder how I feel
light on a face of blues
its mask startled by the truth
of nakedness
and tribal longing.
In each pose the male psyche
stays geometric from head
to negative space to limbs
and a genteel uprising
staged with yellow stripes
across my abdomen
crimson flair at an elbow
ochre outline of one ear
or strands of wild hair
ignited ablaze in pastels
melts my ego
from hunter-gatherer
to artist's muse.

Later, a voluptuous
inner emerald
outward patina gold
touches you, warm naïve lines of me
facing sacred enlightenment.
I claim, through intuited volume
the inner space
true verdant self
in each present moment.
Men wonder how I feel
intimacy sitting

comfortable on the foliage
of my chair
wrapped in flowering tapestry
collective pain dissolved
by a wash of wistful summery leaves.
In every pose
the feminine
oval, open, original
from slightly parted lips
to white space, the black
straps of shoes
then a human bridge
built of lightly shaded legs
rounded ivory knees
angular flattened toes
and fingers, aquamarine
aged, archival
doing the work
connecting the physical
to my spiritual world.

FAMOUS

Headlights lining boulevards like iced lace
Lexus lovers flashing an orange angst
at Fairfax and Fountain, nighttime stares blanks.
Hybrids all humming, we plod along defaced
by each other, windows rolled closed to space
time, claim room. I'm moved by some Mozart pranks
on KUSC, giving quiet thanks
for my ears and heart, I feel I've been graced.
Yet I raise the volume and start to sing
loud, filling my Prius with purple stars
then yellow-golden ones hoping to cause
a change in vocal radiance, all things
nuclear fused making a superstar.
The cars around me burst into applause.

MIDSUMMER'S DAY

It was how our friendship
maidenhair and oak
sat in swift sleeveless shadows
reading Shakespeare, water-colored koi
cooled the bottoms of my feet, your head
on my lap, a white camellia at your chest
unearthed all the verses we needed to hear.

It was how a thousand yellow tulips
watched and protected us, Japanese maples
held the sun in each enlightened
leaf, pink Formosa petals fell
around your frailty and filled
its pockets seeking dewdrops, I read
to you and repeated lines
we craved for merriment
seeking extra days.

It was how
when the afternoon abandoned us
momentary as a sound
hardly ready to go home
we rose holding hands, watched
the camellia fall silent soft
on your footprint, and I knew
you were leaving it for me, offering
everything we had come to learn.

BEING THE ONE

I want to be the one
who invites you to dinner
then lights candles, the one
who puts the spoon next
to a knife, centers plates
and slowly folds the napkin, I want
to be the one who pulls out
your chair, touches your back
and smiles, the one who speaks
of gardens, grows tulips and gladiolas
with hollyhocks, and then becomes
quiet enough like sunlit spring azaleas
to bring charity with handpicked bouquets.
I want to be the one who whispers
about coming health and easy breaths
where they hide and how they will abide.

Life stuns, you know, when it
suddenly does what we didn't expect
taking away, ending, starting again
with changed landscapes. Today we
are lucky as we quietly fold laundry
make a sandwich, walk holding hands
from room to room and share. I am
the one who sees a new moon
cupped between clouds, and expects
you will always know the safety
of camellia petals by palm trees, scattered
showers of pollen, steel gray hillsides
edged with brush and winter dry, night's
first coolness through open windows, scattered
specks of sundown, and faithful worker bees
who crawl inside the mouths of roses ready
to teach us what will likely happen next.

SNOW 1992

It has started now
just as they predicted
blizzard through the night
and I will check each hour
by the streetlamp
for our future.
Your bed shelters
you in an eye
unaware of the storm, breaths
go faster and faster, icy
pneumonia clouds lungs
blocks pathways
and you hurry
though you do not move
outside the fall and rise
of your chest, cold
flaking to your lips.
You tilt your head away
facing what I am not, my
voice freezing, as I
silently find
and huddle
around the warm glow
of a past.
Temperatures fall.
Failing, I zip my coat
in snow piles
surrounding us, roads
become impassable, dim
like the chance
of waking you
finding an escape
rewriting an outcome.

After midnight
I cannot see
the lamp
or the light
of tomorrow's date, only you
drifting, wind and whorl

gasping
the incessant
need
to reach
an end.
When it stops
dawn comes
a white sorrowful
blanket
covering ground
and rooftops, gently
pulled over your body
touching your chin
shrouding
our sweet friendship
blocking
my caress.

THE SOUP WE GIVE

My mother cooks
some chicken soup
from scratch and says
it is good for me
can make me strong.
I remind her,
"Ma, we're not Jewish,"
but the way she shrugs
her shoulders, fights back
with our neighborhood
Brooklyn tongue
and sets the wishbone
on a sill
makes me think
she's one
fine apprentice.
Mom hands
me a bowl
nagging, piercing
through the heavy
kitchen steam.

My mother knows
as she studies
my light green eyes
rubbed and wiped
I am worn out
from losing
so many friends
too many
Angel Food clients
because of AIDS.
I doubt
Kosher foods
can heal this loss.

My mother says,
"When I was a little girl
so many Jewish mothers
in those camps

not able to prepare
a meal, such a waste, do you
want more
hot broth?"
I perk up
she and I
a team
in this room
walls and ceilings
stained
by whispered recipes
and spoken prayers.
She is by birth
an understudy
but I am
by nature
a main character
surviving
to agitate
flesh out roles
and deliver food.
I stand by
the stove
and watch her
stir.
"Don't you think, Ma, this pot
needs some more
cayenne pepper?"

HE'S THE ONE (THEY DON'T KNOW I'M YOUR BOYFRIEND)

I want
no more lies
no sabotaging
self-talk, you've
taught me
how to get Black
now when pushed
too far
by prejudice
and ignorance
just watch
how we take
your wheelchair
and get naked
to enjoy
the erotic moves
of disabled sex
cerebral palsied pleasures
and the success
of our bodies
sweating
youthful yet again
then afterwards
laughing
to ourselves
I push, you roll
outside
for some cool
air and enhanced
smell of our
night-blooming
jasmine, neighbors
walking by
smile approvingly
as they assume
I'm your caretaker
but I grin
nod back
and whisper

under my breath
no, he's my lover
and in fact
when we're
together
he walks
on water.

AFTER OUR NAP

Eucalyptus leaves
level stillness on the ground
air becomes more pure
thanks to artists
breathing deeply
in this park.
Our blanket softens
twisted tree roots
and the dry earth beneath
as we open our eyes
to familiar late day clouds.

You can begin now
with indigo and white pastel
across the top
of cream-colored paper.
Your blue absorbs the daylight
as it spreads background
and supports growing limbs
from top branches
to sandy cocoa earth
you draw below.
You work bottom and sides
margins by edges
winding emerald moss
and mustard ivy
around trunks
and faces of angular rocks.
Seagulls circling
our heads
send caws into the purples
of your uneven grasses.

Afternoon bright
begins to fade
casting tangelo
shadows everywhere.
You grab some
with a crayon
and splash it

onto your sky
like fire
without flames
heat causing dusk.
I nervously begin
to search
the ground at our feet
while darkness arrives
until finally
there it is
the tiny
pale glowworm
we dreamed about
hours ago.
With my finger
I rub yellow light
from its body, transfer
some to your drawing
beneath the perfect
flat silver stones
and then
your artwork
is properly signed.

YOGA AT BEDTIME

The night garden is silent while flowers nod dew
drops onto leaves, beryl stems bend and bob

to the inhale, exhale of slow postures
lotus legs beneath each chant.

A yoga teacher, back straight and raw
as carrots digging downward to fulfillment

lives in my head and foresees with eyes closed
the greening of tomorrow's kale

healing of arthritis along a spine
and wide opening of snapdragons' mouths

in the backyard we've shared for thirty years.
Headstands happened here decades ago

vacations to Hollywood turned into this home with plantable land.
Being young and from New Jersey

what did we know about the Left Coast and love
sitting forward bends or mountain poses?

Our story was as one day at a time
as living happily ever after.

Still, Birds of paradise welcomed us with titian and navy smiles
like a Mamas and Papa's song come true

proving transplants can somehow just take root
among grafted lemon trees, hybrid tea roses, or Darwin tulips.

Evenings now, relaxation poses help me find order among the chaos.
For us, a downward dog is followed by a sunrise

heirloom tomatoes grow deepest red
when rotated with beans and yellow onions

and Haas avocadoes picked at midnight taste buttery
on sourdough toast the next morning.

This night, after a circle knee child's pose
teacher nudges me and it's time for bed

we gratefully go upstairs
to sleep like Zen Masters in Training.

OUT WEST

I have no angst to give you
no purgatory edge
I'm old, I've seen too much
and besides
in California we wear light
colors inside our clothes
year round
no rain
so take, for example
cancer in remission
my partner's oscillating cells healthy
no longer stalked
he patiently lives
beneath palms
praying for his wholeness
few can imagine how
walking and running
or flying with more
than just arms and hands
can only happen in his most midnight dreams
the thing is
he never complains
not even his eyes
because Angelinos, we're all about
the re-inventing
or well
at least the acting as-if.
He knows
it's not the words you say
when you pray
but the spin
comes within and without.
Every morning I trace
his face with my fingertips
and tell him he looks
more and more like his mother
lands of Senegal, Ghana,
Cameroon,
and so he has work to do

stories to tell
because they run
and push
through his blood.

WHAT WE KNOW

Bullies are assholes. I mean
by the time I reached 70
I understood them
for what they did, the ones
who wore pink power ties
and fake suntans, the ones
who talked like a grand dragon
sheriff with bloodspots
on his badge, the ones
who looked you in the eye
and smiled as they cheated, the ones
who were smug as they voted
against your rights, the ones
who shot my body
full of shame, riddled my brain
with gossip and blame, wounded
my psyche again and again.
I writhed a little longer
in the lies, then found this way
to speak the truth
and move on.

At night I listen to the sounds
of dreams rise
from my partner
sleeping next to me, interracial
hands clasp beneath
a family quilt, the mindful moon
of midnight stand watch
outside our bedroom windows, as I
count the years
we've been together
falling
gently falling
into the next day
and the next
everything to make me
feel safe
everything.

THIS ADULT

We always want something
a red Schwinn bicycle
or prize bonsai tree
the perfect job
and invitations to dinner
the tools to be transcendent
so we're recognized and remembered
glow after dark
and even though
those wants often change appearance
grow bigger
the thrill
their frill lining the palms
of my hands
smooths away
and I
am still me
small
the singular and puzzled
boy
half-smiling
for a photo
telling my name
and how old I am
playing until bedtime
and then kissing
my mother goodnight
my father, sweet dreams
steadily wondering
how I'll ever become
who
they want me
to be.

END

hands wrinkled, skin paper-thin, transparent
voice vibrates weak across hairless skull, I keep my promise
raising your names each day, holding memories inside a breath
who will speak of you when I'm gone

voice vibrates weak across hairless skull, I keep my promise
the men I lost hardest to AIDS
who will speak of you when I'm gone
Loren, Nick, Kevin, George, Russell, Kim

the men I lost hardest to AIDS
partner, best friends, neighbors
Loren, Nick, Kevin, George, Russell, Kim
longed to go with you, not knowing what else to do

partner, best friends, neighbors
today we're finally together again
longed to go with you, not knowing what else to do
I wrote death poems, prayer after prayer, at your bedsides

today we're finally together again
sitting in a soft chair, frail, drifting, spirited
I wrote death poems, prayer after prayer, at your bedsides
this one is for me, out of breath, out of time

sitting in a soft chair, frail, drifting, spirited
I see your faces, reach for your hands
this one is for me, out of breath, out of time
who will speak of us when I'm gone

www.ingramcontent.com/pod-product-compliance
Lightning Source LLC
Chambersburg PA
CBHW022123090426
42743CB00008B/973